Those Who Dare To

Wrestle With The Divine God

Alternative Perceptions Of The Word We Live In,

Inspired By The Wisdom Of Dr. Jordan B. Peterson

Steven Ben Richardson

Content

PART I: FOUNDATIONS OF DIVINE WRESTLING

Chapter 1: The Nature of Divine Wrestling

The Origins of Sacred Struggle

The word "Israel" holds a secret at its core - it means "those who wrestle with God." This ancient name, born from Jacob's mysterious nighttime struggle by the river Jabbok, sets the foundation for understanding our relationship with the divine. When Jordan Peterson first encountered this translation during his biblical lectures in 2017, it changed his entire perspective on religious experience. The concept of wrestling with God - rather than merely believing in or submitting to God - opened up new ways of understanding human consciousness and our search for meaning. The psychological weight of this divine wrestling manifests itself in every serious conversation about faith, doubt, and meaning. In Peterson's clinical practice and academic work at the University of Toronto, he observed how individuals who engaged actively with their beliefs - who dared to question, to doubt, to struggle - often developed stronger psychological foundations than those who accepted without questioning.

Historical Patterns of Divine Confrontation

Throughout recorded history, humans have documented their confrontations with the divine. The Mesopotamian Epic of Gilgamesh shows the hero challenging the gods. The Greek myth of Prometheus depicts direct defiance of divine authority. But it's in the Jewish tradition where we find the most sustained examination of this spiritual wrestling match.

The story of Abraham questioning God about the fate of Sodom and Gomorrah demonstrates this tradition. Moses argues with God at the burning bush, presenting his doubts and fears. Job refuses to accept simple answers about his suffering, maintaining his integrity while demanding answers from God. These aren't mere stories of rebellion - they represent a sophisticated understanding of how humans relate to the transcendent.

The Transformative Power of Sacred Conflict

Peterson's clinical work revealed a pattern: individuals who engaged in genuine spiritual struggle often emerged stronger, more integrated, and more capable of handling life's challenges. This mirrors the biblical account of Jacob, who emerged from his wrestling match with both a limp and a blessing - transformed by his encounter with the divine.

In Peterson's lectures at Harvard and the University of Toronto, he emphasized how this pattern of transformation through struggle appears consistently across cultures. The Native American vision quest, Buddhist meditation practices, and Christian contemplative traditions all incorporate elements of spiritual wrestling that lead to personal transformation.

Sacred Wrestling in Modern Times

The relevance of divine wrestling hasn't diminished in our technological age. Peterson's observations during his clinical practice showed that modern individuals still face the same fundamental questions about meaning, purpose, and their relationship with the transcendent. The difference lies in our framework for understanding these struggles.

When Peterson spoke at Oxford in 2018, he noted that our contemporary psychological challenges often mask deeper spiritual questions. The anxiety about career choices, relationships, and personal identity that brings people to therapy often reflects a deeper wrestling with fundamental questions of meaning and purpose.

Modern therapeutic practices, as Peterson observed, sometimes try to eliminate struggle altogether, offering quick solutions and comfort. However, his work suggests that engaging in the struggle itself - much like Jacob's wrestling match - might be essential for psychological and spiritual growth.

The Cost and Reward of Divine Combat

Peterson's extensive study of historical religious traditions reveals a consistent theme: divine wrestling carries both cost and reward. Jacob's limp symbolizes how genuine spiritual engagement often leaves permanent marks. Yet these marks become badges of authenticity, signs of real engagement with life's deepest questions.

In his clinical practice, Peterson noticed that patients who avoided spiritual struggles often encountered more severe psychological difficulties later. Those who engaged in the wrestling match - who questioned their beliefs, confronted their doubts, and challenged their assumptions - developed stronger psychological resources for handling life's challenges.

Alignment with Natural Order

The concept of wrestling with God takes on additional significance when considered alongside Peterson's observations about natural hierarchies and order. His research indicates that this spiritual struggle might serve as a natural organizing principle for human consciousness, helping individuals align themselves with deeper patterns of meaning and order in the universe.

Through his years of treating patients and studying religious traditions, Peterson identified how this wrestling process often follows predictable patterns. It begins with a confrontation with mystery or suffering, proceeds through stages of questioning and struggle, and potentially leads to a new integration of personality and belief.

The Psychological Structure of Divine Wrestling

Peterson's research into the psychological components of religious experience sheds light on why divine wrestling appears across cultures and throughout history. The act of wrestling with God engages multiple levels of human consciousness - intellectual, emotional, and what Carl Jung called the collective unconscious.

This process activates fundamental psychological structures that Peterson studied extensively during his academic career. The archetypal patterns of hero, dragon, and divine father all play roles in this spiritual combat, creating a psychological drama that engages our deepest mental structures.

Wrestling as Revolutionary Act

In Peterson's analysis, the very act of wrestling with God represents a revolutionary stance toward existence itself. Rather than passive acceptance or outright rejection, it suggests a third way - active engagement with the deepest questions of being. This approach aligns with Peterson's observations about the relationship between responsibility and meaning in human life.

Chapter 2: The Architecture of Belief

The Structure of Faith

When Jordan Peterson began teaching at Harvard University in 1993, he noticed something remarkable about his students' reactions to religious discussions. Those who claimed to reject religious belief still organized their lives around central values and meaning structures that mirrored religious frameworks. This observation led Peterson to spend five years writing "Maps of Meaning: The Architecture of Belief," published in 1999.

The book arose from Peterson's attempt to understand the psychological foundations of belief systems. Through his research at McGill

University and Harvard, Peterson identified how belief systems form the basic architecture of human consciousness. These systems don't simply exist as abstract ideas - they manifest in neural pathways, behavioral patterns, and social structures.

In his University of Toronto lectures, Peterson demonstrated how belief systems act as filters through which humans perceive reality. Each person carries an internal map - not just of physical geography, but of moral and metaphysical territory. These maps determine what we notice, what we value, and how we act.

Scientific Foundations of Sacred Experience

Peterson's work at Harvard focused on the neuropsychology of religious and ideological belief. His research showed how religious experiences activate specific brain regions associated with meaning-making and emotional regulation. These findings aligned with studies conducted at the Douglas Hospital during his post-doctoral fellowship.

During his lectures at the University of Toronto, Peterson explained how modern neuroscience supports ancient religious insights. The brain's default mode network - active during self-reflection and moral reasoning - shows increased activity during religious contemplation. This scientific observation matches the religious notion that humans naturally seek meaning and transcendent truth.

Peterson's research demonstrated that religious myths and scientific facts aren't opposing forces - they represent different levels of analysis. Religious stories describe patterns of human behavior and experience that science can measure but cannot fully explain through materialistic reduction alone.

The Power of Ancient Patterns

Through his clinical practice in Montreal and Toronto, Peterson observed how mythological patterns emerge spontaneously in dreams and psychological crises. These patterns match what Carl Jung called archetypes - universal symbols and story elements that appear across cultures and throughout history.

Peterson's examination of religious texts revealed recurring symbolic patterns. The hero who faces chaos, the wise old man, the great mother - these figures appear not just in stories but in how people naturally organize their understanding of life. His lectures at Harvard demonstrated how these patterns manifest in literature, art, and personal narratives. The archetypal patterns Peterson studied aren't arbitrary cultural inventions. They reflect fundamental psychological structures that helped humans survive and thrive throughout history. His research showed how these patterns still shape modern human behavior, even among people who reject traditional religious frameworks.

Neurobiology of Transcendence

When Peterson conducted research at McGill University's Douglas Hospital, he studied how altered states of consciousness affect human perception and behavior. His work revealed that transcendent experiences - whether induced through meditation, prayer, or psychedelics - create measurable changes in brain function.

These experiences, Peterson noted in his Harvard lectures, often lead to lasting personality changes. People who undergo genuine transcendent experiences typically show increased openness to experience and decreased anxiety. The brain scans of long-term meditators show structural changes in areas associated with self-awareness and emotional regulation.

Peterson's clinical practice provided numerous examples of how transcendent experiences can catalyze psychological transformation. However, he emphasized that these experiences must be integrated into daily life through practical action to create lasting positive change.

The Maps We Live By

Through his psychological practice, Peterson documented how people navigate life using internal maps of meaning. These maps aren't just intellectual constructs - they're embedded in emotion, instinct, and behavior. When these maps fail, people experience psychological crisis.

Peterson's research at the University of Toronto showed how belief systems serve as navigation tools for life's challenges. People with well-developed belief systems show greater resilience in facing adversity. Their internal maps help them make decisions and find meaning in difficult circumstances.

The effectiveness of these belief systems doesn't depend on their literal truth, but on their practical value in organizing experience and guiding behavior. Peterson's clinical work demonstrated how functional belief systems must bridge between physical reality and transcendent values.

Biological Roots of Belief

Peterson's research into evolutionary psychology revealed how belief systems emerge from biological necessities. Humans needed reliable ways to coordinate behavior and maintain social order. Religious and ideological systems provided frameworks for this coordination.

In his University of Toronto lectures, Peterson explained how belief systems helped humans manage uncertainty and anxiety. The brain creates meaning structures as naturally as it creates visual images from sensory input. These meaning structures became increasingly sophisticated as human societies developed. Peterson's work showed how religious beliefs aren't simply cultural additions to human nature - they're expressions of fundamental psychological needs and capacities. His research indicated that humans are naturally religious, not in terms of specific doctrines, but in their need for meaning and transcendent values.

The Architecture of Personal Transformation

Through his clinical practice, Peterson observed how personal transformation follows predictable patterns. These patterns mirror religious stories of death and rebirth, suggesting that religious narratives capture fundamental truths about psychological development.

His work at Harvard demonstrated how personal growth often requires the death of old belief systems and the birth of new ones. This process creates psychological turbulence but can lead to greater stability and maturity. Peterson's research showed how this pattern repeats across cultures and throughout individual lives.

Chapter 3: Order and Chaos in Divine Dialogue

The Dance of Opposites

In the University of Toronto's psychology department, Jordan Peterson spent twenty years studying how humans handle the fundamental opposition between order and chaos. His research revealed that this duality appears in every major religious tradition - from the Chinese concept of yin and yang to the Biblical separation of light from darkness in Genesis. Through his clinical practice, Peterson observed how this duality manifests in individual lives. His patients often arrived at his office when their orderly world had collapsed - after job losses, divorces, or health crises. These moments of chaos, while painful, often preceded periods of significant personal growth. During his lectures at Harvard, Peterson explained how the human brain processes order and chaos differently. The left hemisphere specializes in maintaining known categories and structures, while the right hemisphere excels at detecting anomalies and processing novel situations. This neurological split reflects the ancient religious understanding of reality's dual nature.

The Nature of Sacred Balance

Peterson's extensive study of religious texts revealed how different traditions approach the balance between order and chaos. The Ancient Egyptians represented this through the gods Horus and Seth. The Greeks expressed it through Apollo and Dionysus. These weren't merely stories - they represented psychological truths that Peterson encountered repeatedly in his clinical work. At the University of Toronto, Peterson's research demonstrated how mental health depends on maintaining proper balance between stability and change. Too much order leads to stagnation and tyranny. Too much chaos creates anxiety and depression. The sweet spot lies in between - what he called "meaningful order." His work with patients showed how this balance plays out in real life. Those who avoided all chaos became rigid and unable to adapt. Those who rejected all order fell into nihilism and despair. Health meant learning to stand with one foot in order and one in chaos.

Sacred Acts of Creation

During his time teaching at Harvard, Peterson studied how humans create order from chaos. His research showed that this creative process invariably involves sacrifice - giving up one possibility to actualize another. This psychological truth appears in religious stories worldwide, from Abraham's near-sacrifice of Isaac to the dismemberment of Osiris.

Peterson's clinical practice provided numerous examples of how sacrifice creates order. Patients who successfully rebuilt their lives after a crisis had to give up old habits, relationships, or beliefs. The sacrifice wasn't just symbolic - it required real loss for new growth to occur.

In his University of Toronto lectures, Peterson explained how sacrifice operates at both individual and social levels. Societies maintain order through agreed-upon sacrifices - giving up immediate gratification for long-term stability. When these sacrificial systems break down, social chaos follows.

The Unknown Territory

Through years of treating patients, Peterson witnessed how people react when facing the unknown. His research showed that humans share universal responses to uncertainty - increased heart rate, heightened alertness, and activation of ancient survival mechanisms in the brain.

At McGill University, Peterson's early research focused on how alcohol affects risk assessment and response to uncertainty. This work revealed fundamental patterns in how humans cope with the unknown. Some people freeze, others flee, while others face the uncertainty head-on.

Peterson's examination of religious texts showed how different traditions provide tools for handling uncertainty. The Bible describes this through stories of wilderness wandering. Buddhist texts discuss it through concepts of emptiness. These ancient wisdom traditions align with modern psychological insights about managing anxiety and fear.

Patterns of Transformation

Peterson's research at the University of Toronto revealed consistent patterns in how people transform chaos into order. This process follows stages similar to the hero's myth described by Joseph Campbell - a confrontation with chaos, a death of the old self, and a rebirth into new order.

His clinical work demonstrated these patterns in action. Patients who successfully transformed their lives went through predictable stages. First came disorientation as old structures collapsed.

Then came a period of active engagement with chaos. Finally, new order emerged through conscious effort and sacrifice.

The Price of Creation

During his lectures on biblical stories, Peterson emphasized how creating order always comes at a price. His psychological research confirmed this ancient wisdom. Establishing new patterns requires energy, attention, and the sacrifice of comfortable but outdated ways of being. Peterson's clinical experience showed how people often resist paying this price. They remain in dysfunction rather than face the pain of transformation. Yet those who accepted the cost and moved forward consistently reported greater satisfaction and meaning in their lives.

PART II: THE HERO'S JOURNEY THROUGH DIVINITY

Chapter 4: The Call to Adventure

Signs and Signals

Jordan Peterson's work at the University of Toronto brought him face-to-face with students experiencing what religious traditions call "the call." In his clinical practice, patients often described moments when their ordinary lives cracked open, revealing possibilities they had never considered. These experiences matched the patterns Peterson studied in religious texts - particularly the story of Moses at the burning bush and Abraham's midnight summons.

In his Harvard lectures, Peterson described how these calls often arrive during periods of apparent stability. His research showed that people typically receive their strongest impulses toward transformation not when they're in crisis, but when they're settled into comfortable routines. This observation aligned with the biblical pattern - Abraham was wealthy and established when God called him to leave everything behind.

The Moment of Decision

Through his years of clinical practice, Peterson witnessed how people respond to life-altering moments of choice. Some patients recognized these moments immediately and acted with courage. Others hesitated, rationalized, or turned away completely. His observations proved that the ancient religious stories about refusing divine calls weren't mere myths - they described real psychological processes. Peterson's research at McGill University examined how people make decisions under pressure. His findings showed that humans often default to maintaining current patterns, even when those patterns cause suffering. This tendency explains why biblical figures like Jonah initially ran from their calling, and why modern individuals often resist opportunities for growth.

The Cost of Refusal

At the University of Toronto, Peterson's studies revealed the psychological consequences of refusing authentic calls to growth. His clinical practice provided numerous examples of people who, having recognized a need for change, chose instead to remain in familiar patterns. The results consistently included increased anxiety, depression, and what Peterson termed "existential angst." These observations matched the religious patterns Peterson studied in ancient texts. The story of Jonah illustrated how refusing a legitimate call leads to psychological descent - represented in the myth by Jonah's time in the belly of the whale. Peterson's patients often described similar feelings of being "swallowed up" by life after turning away from necessary changes.

The Elements of Preparation

Peterson's research showed how proper preparation determines success in major life transitions. During his time at Harvard, he studied how individuals successfully managed radical life changes. The pattern required specific elements: clear goals, realistic assessments of current capabilities, and carefully structured plans for developing necessary skills. His clinical work demonstrated how unprepared individuals often failed in their attempts at transformation. This matched the religious pattern of preparation seen in biblical narratives - Moses spent years in Midian before leading the Exodus, David served as a shepherd before becoming king. Peterson's research revealed that similar periods of preparation remain necessary for modern transformations.

The Structure of Support

Through his psychological practice, Peterson observed how successful personal transformation requires adequate support systems. His studies showed that individuals attempting major life changes without proper guidance typically failed, while those who found appropriate mentors and support networks succeeded more often. This finding aligned with Peterson's analysis of religious initiation rites, which always include experienced guides who have walked the path before. His work demonstrated that this ancient wisdom about the necessity of guides remains valid in modern contexts. The brain itself, Peterson noted in his lectures, responds differently to challenges when we have trusted guides versus facing them alone.

Recognizing False Calls

Peterson's clinical experience revealed how often people mistake impulses for authentic calls. His research identified specific patterns that distinguished genuine opportunities for growth from what he called "sirens of destruction." This work proved valuable in helping patients distinguish between legitimate callings and self-destructive urges.

In his biblical lectures, Peterson explained how religious traditions address this issue through stories of false prophets and deceptive spirits. His psychological research showed that these ancient warnings described real phenomena - the human tendency to mistake momentary impulses for genuine calls to transformation.

Chapter 5: Confronting the Dragon of Chaos

The Face of Fear

During his years as a clinical psychologist, Jordan Peterson encountered hundreds of patients facing their personal dragons. These weren't mythical creatures, but real psychological barriers that prevented growth and progress. Through his work at the University of Toronto, Peterson documented how these internal obstacles manifest in specific, measurable ways: increased heart rate, elevated cortisol levels, and distinctive patterns of brain activation.

In his lectures at Harvard, Peterson explained how ancient myths about dragon-slaying contained psychological truths his research had confirmed. The dragon, he noted, appears in every major cultural tradition - from the Norse Jörmungandr to the Biblical Leviathan. These weren't mere storytelling conveniences. They represented patterns of threat and response hardwired into the human nervous system.

The Anatomy of Internal Monsters

Peterson's research at McGill University focused on how people identify and confront their greatest challenges. His clinical work revealed that personal dragons often wear familiar faces: addiction, procrastination, resentment, and fear. These weren't abstract concepts but measurable patterns of behavior and thought that his patients had to overcome. Through careful observation in his clinical practice, Peterson identified how these internal monsters develop. Each patient's story revealed similar patterns - small compromises that grew into major obstacles, avoided responsibilities that became overwhelming barriers, and unacknowledged resentments that transformed into seemingly insurmountable walls.

The Biology of Confrontation

At the University of Toronto, Peterson studied the physiological responses of individuals facing significant life challenges. His research showed how confronting personal dragons triggers ancient survival mechanisms in the brain. The sympathetic nervous system activates, stress hormones flood the bloodstream, and cognitive patterns shift toward threat assessment.

These biological responses, Peterson noted in his lectures, match the physical descriptions in ancient hero myths. The trembling, sweating, and racing heart of the mythical hero weren't literary flourishes - they were accurate descriptions of how humans respond to genuine challenges. His clinical observations confirmed these same physical reactions in patients facing their personal dragons.

The Price of Avoidance

Through years of clinical practice, Peterson documented the costs of avoiding necessary confrontations. His patients who repeatedly backed away from challenges developed predictable patterns of psychological deterioration: increasing anxiety, depression, and what he termed "existential angst."

This matched the patterns Peterson found in religious and mythological texts. The hero who refuses the call, who runs from the dragon, invariably faces worse consequences than the one who turns to fight. His research showed how this ancient wisdom reflected psychological reality - avoidance of necessary challenges leads to greater suffering, not less.

The Nature of True Courage

Peterson's work with patients revealed how genuine courage differs from its popular representations. In his Harvard lectures, he explained that true courage isn't the absence of fear but the willingness to act despite it. His clinical observations showed how this principle played out in real situations.

His research demonstrated that successful confrontations with personal dragons followed specific patterns. Patients who overcame their challenges didn't wait for fear to disappear. Instead, they developed strategies for functioning effectively while experiencing fear. This aligned with the heroic patterns Peterson studied in mythology - the hero trembles but acts anyway.

The Mechanics of Transformation

Through his psychological practice, Peterson observed how people transform through confrontation with their personal dragons. His research showed that meaningful change requires specific elements: clear recognition of the challenge, acceptance of responsibility, and willingness to endure temporary discomfort for long-term gain. These observations aligned with the structure of hero myths Peterson studied. The hero must first see the dragon clearly, accept the task of confronting it, and endure the battle's hardships. His clinical work confirmed that modern psychological transformations follow similar patterns.

The Territory of Transformation

In Peterson's clinical observations at the University of Toronto, he noticed how confrontation with personal dragons changes people physically. His patients who successfully faced their challenges showed measurable differences in posture, voice tone, and even facial expressions. These weren't superficial changes - brain scans revealed altered neural patterns in people who had overcome significant personal obstacles.

During his biblical lectures, Peterson connected these observations to ancient wisdom about transformation through struggle. The story of

Jacob wrestling with the angel especially interested him - Jacob emerged with a limp but also a blessing. Peterson's clinical work showed similar patterns: patients often carried scars from their battles, but these marks became signs of strength rather than weakness.

The Science of Struggle

Peterson's research at McGill University examined the neurological basis of meaningful struggle. His studies showed how challenging experiences literally rewire the brain, creating new neural pathways and strengthening existing ones. This scientific finding supported what religious traditions had long claimed - that struggle against worthy opponents creates positive change. His work revealed how the brain responds differently to meaningful versus meaningless challenges. When people engage in struggles they consider worthwhile, their bodies release different combinations of neurochemicals than when facing random stress. This physiological distinction helps explain why some forms of suffering lead to growth while others cause damage.

Wounds and Wisdom

Through his psychological practice, Peterson documented how wounds received in meaningful struggles differ from other injuries. His patients who fought their personal dragons often emerged stronger, despite - and sometimes because of - their scars. This observation led to his research into post-traumatic growth, a phenomenon where people become stronger through adversity. His studies at the University of Toronto demonstrated how this process works. When people voluntarily confront difficulties, their nervous systems respond differently than when facing random trauma. The voluntary nature of the confrontation changes how the brain processes the experience, often leading to increased resilience rather than increased vulnerability.

The Power of Recognition

Peterson's clinical work showed the importance of recognizing genuine achievement. His patients who successfully confronted their dragons needed their victories acknowledged - not through empty praise, but through genuine recognition of their accomplishment. This observation connected to his studies of initiation rites in traditional societies, where communities formally recognized individuals who had faced significant challenges. His research revealed how proper recognition of achievement affects brain chemistry. Success acknowledged by others triggers different neural responses than solitary accomplishment. This finding explained why traditional societies always celebrated hero's returns publicly - social recognition helps consolidate personal transformation.

The Cycle of Growth

At Harvard, Peterson's research examined how personal transformation creates ripple effects. His clinical observations showed that people who successfully confronted one dragon often became better equipped to face others. Each victory, however small, changed both the person and their relationship to future challenges.

His studies demonstrated how this cycle works neurologically. Each successful confrontation with a personal dragon alters brain structure, making future confrontations more manageable. This scientific finding supported the ancient wisdom that heroes become more capable through successive challenges.

The Social Dimension

Peterson's work revealed how personal dragons often have social components. His clinical practice showed that individual transformation affects entire social networks. When one person successfully confronted their dragons, it often inspired others to face their own challenges.

This observation connected to Peterson's analysis of religious texts, where individual heroic acts frequently led to broader social transformation. His research showed how this pattern continues today - personal courage often catalyzes positive changes in families, workplaces, and larger communities.

Chapter 6: The Sacred Marriage of Opposites

The Shadow Within

At the University of Toronto, Jordan Peterson studied how people confront and integrate their darker aspects. His clinical practice revealed patterns in how individuals deal with what Carl Jung called "the shadow" - those parts of ourselves we prefer not to acknowledge. Peterson's observations showed that people who refused to recognize their shadow aspects often projected them onto others, creating unnecessary conflicts and social problems.

Through his psychological practice, Peterson documented how shadow integration actually works. His patients who successfully incorporated their darker aspects showed measurable improvements in psychological health. Brain scans revealed increased activity in areas associated with emotional regulation and self-awareness when people acknowledged rather than suppressed their shadow elements.

The Dance of Darkness and Light

Peterson's research at Harvard examined how successful integration of opposing forces occurs in the psyche. His studies showed that mental health requires acknowledgment and incorporation of both light and dark aspects of personality. This finding aligned with religious traditions Peterson studied, particularly the Taoist concept of yin and yang.

His clinical work demonstrated how this integration process affects behavior. Patients who accepted their full range of capabilities - including aggressive and competitive impulses - showed better outcomes than those who tried to maintain an artificially positive self-image. This observation supported ancient wisdom about the necessity of incorporating rather than denying darker aspects of human nature.

The Divine Mirror

During his lectures on biblical stories, Peterson explained how religious texts describe the process of reconciliation with higher meaning. His research showed how this reconciliation occurs psychologically through acceptance of personal limitation and recognition of transcendent value. The biblical story of Job particularly interested him as an example of this process. His clinical observations revealed similar patterns in modern individuals. Patients who maintained connection with something greater than themselves - whether religious faith or secular values - showed better resilience in facing life's challenges. Their brain activity displayed patterns associated with reduced anxiety and increased sense of meaning.

Male and Female Principles

Peterson's extensive research into gender differences revealed consistent patterns across cultures. His work showed how masculine and feminine principles manifest in psychology, regardless of an individual's biological sex. These findings helped explain why ancient myths consistently portrayed psychological wholeness as a marriage of masculine and feminine elements. Through his clinical practice, Peterson observed how integration of masculine and feminine qualities creates psychological balance. His patients who successfully incorporated both assertiveness (traditionally masculine) and receptivity (traditionally feminine) showed better outcomes in relationships and career success.

The Archetypal Union

At McGill University, Peterson studied how archetypal patterns influence human behavior. His research revealed that the marriage of opposites appears as a central theme across cultures because it reflects fundamental psychological truths. This pattern shows up in religious symbols worldwide - from the Hindu Shiva-Shakti to the Christian Holy Spirit as mediator between Father and Son.

His clinical work demonstrated how these archetypal patterns manifest in modern life.

Patients who recognized and worked with these patterns showed faster progress than those who approached their problems purely rationally. This observation supported Peterson's argument that ancient wisdom contains practical psychological truth.

PART III: PRACTICAL APPLICATIONS OF DIVINE WRESTLING

Chapter 7: The Individual and the Divine

The Psychology of Personal Responsibility

In Peterson's clinical practice, he observed a direct correlation between acceptance of personal responsibility and psychological health. His patients who took ownership of their circumstances, regardless of external factors, showed measurable improvements in mental well-being. Brain scans revealed increased activity in areas associated with executive function when individuals actively embraced responsibility rather than avoiding it.

At the University of Toronto, Peterson's research demonstrated how personal responsibility activates specific neural pathways. When individuals accept responsibility for their actions, the prefrontal cortex shows increased activity, while denial of responsibility correlates with activation in the amygdala - the brain's fear center. This neurological evidence supports ancient wisdom about the psychological benefits of taking responsibility.

The Neuroscience of Character Development

Peterson's studies at McGill University examined the biological basis of character development. His research revealed how repeated choices create neural pathways that become increasingly automatic over time. This finding explained the psychological mechanism behind character formation - each decision literally shapes the physical structure of the brain. His clinical observations showed how this process works in real time. Patients who consistently made difficult but ethical choices developed stronger neural connections in regions associated with self-control and moral reasoning. This strengthening process mirrors the religious concept of building character through moral choices.

Truth as Psychological Medicine

Through his therapeutic practice, Peterson documented the psychological effects of truthful speech. His research showed how telling lies, even small ones, activates stress responses in the body, while speaking truth reduces physiological markers of anxiety. This finding provided scientific support for religious teachings about the healing power of truth.

At Harvard, Peterson studied how truth-telling affects brain chemistry. His research revealed that honest self-expression triggers the release of neurochemicals associated with well-being, while deception increases cortisol levels and activates stress responses. These physiological effects explain why truth-telling forms such a central part of psychological healing.

The Foundation of Meaning

Peterson's clinical work revealed consistent patterns in how individuals construct meaningful lives. His research showed that meaning emerges from the acceptance of responsibility, the pursuit of truth, and engagement with challenges that foster growth. These elements appeared repeatedly in successful therapeutic outcomes. His studies demonstrated how meaning manifests neurologically. When individuals engage in purposeful activities, their brains show activation patterns associated with reward and satisfaction. These patterns differ significantly from those seen during mere pleasure-seeking activities, supporting the distinction between happiness and meaning.

The Science of Sacred Space

At the University of Toronto, Peterson researched how humans create and maintain psychological sacred spaces. His work showed that certain mental states - characterized by focused attention and ethical awareness - produce measurable changes in brain activity. These states mirror what religious traditions call sacred consciousness.

His clinical observations revealed how individuals who maintain these psychological sacred spaces show greater resilience in facing life's challenges. Brain scans indicated increased integration between emotional and rational centers during these states, suggesting improved psychological functioning.

Psychological Integration

Peterson's research identified specific patterns in how individuals integrate different aspects of their personalities. His clinical work showed that psychological health requires balanced development of multiple capacities: analytical thinking, emotional awareness, moral reasoning, and behavioral control.

Through careful observation of therapeutic outcomes, Peterson documented how this integration process occurs. Patients who successfully developed these various capacities showed improved relationships, better career outcomes, and increased life satisfaction. Their brain scans revealed greater connectivity between different neural networks.

Chapter 8: Community and Sacred Order

The Psychological Power of Ritual

Through his clinical practice at the University of Toronto, Peterson studied how ritualistic behaviors affect mental health. His research revealed that regular rituals - from simple morning routines to religious ceremonies - create measurable changes in brain chemistry. These changes include reduced cortisol levels and increased production of neurotransmitters associated with well-being.

Peterson's observations showed how ritual practices strengthen neural pathways associated with self-control and emotional regulation. His patients who maintained consistent ritual practices demonstrated better stress management abilities and improved psychological stability. These findings supported traditional psychological theories about the stabilizing effects of ritual behavior.

Neurological Basis of Social Bonds

At McGill University, Peterson's research examined how social connections form at a neurological level. His studies revealed that group participation in meaningful activities triggers the release of oxytocin and other bonding hormones. These biochemical changes strengthen social ties and create lasting neural patterns that support community cohesion.

His clinical work demonstrated how shared beliefs and practices affect brain function. When people participate in group activities they find meaningful, their brains show synchronized patterns of activation. This neural synchronization helps explain why communal practices have such powerful effects on psychological health.

The Architecture of Social Stability

Peterson's research at Harvard focused on how stable social structures develop and maintain themselves. His studies showed that successful communities follow specific psychological principles - clear boundaries, shared values, and predictable consequences for behavior. These elements create what neuroscientists call "social safety networks" in the brain.

Through his therapeutic practice, Peterson documented how these principles affect individual mental health. Patients who belonged to well-structured communities showed better recovery rates from psychological difficulties than those who lacked strong social connections. Their brain scans revealed improved integration between emotional and rational centers.

Leadership and Neural Networks

During his time at the University of Toronto, Peterson studied the psychological characteristics of effective leadership. His research showed how leaders who combine competence with ethical behavior create stronger group cohesion than those who rely on dominance alone. This finding supported traditional teachings about the importance of moral authority in leadership. His clinical observations revealed how good leadership affects group psychology. Communities with ethical, competent leaders showed better mental health outcomes among members. The presence of trusted leadership reduced stress responses and increased cooperative behaviors among group members.

The Biology of Belonging

Peterson's research demonstrated how social belonging affects physical and mental health. His studies showed that social isolation creates patterns of brain activation similar to physical pain, while meaningful group membership reduces stress responses and improves immune function.

Through his clinical practice, Peterson observed how social connections affect recovery from psychological trauma. Patients with strong community ties showed faster improvement rates and better long-term outcomes than those without social support. These observations aligned with traditional wisdom about the healing power of community.

Psychological Foundations of Social Order

Peterson's studies at the University of Toronto revealed how social order emerges from psychological patterns. His research showed that stable communities develop through consistent reinforcement of shared values and behaviors. This process creates neural networks that support social cooperation and mutual understanding.

In his clinical practice, Peterson observed how social order affects individual psychology. People who lived in well-ordered communities displayed lower rates of anxiety and depression. Their brains showed increased activity in regions associated with security and social connection, while areas linked to threat detection showed reduced activation.

The Neural Basis of Social Harmony

Through his research at McGill University, Peterson examined how social harmony develops at a neurological level. His studies revealed that when people engage in cooperative activities, their brains begin to synchronize in measurable ways. This synchronization strengthens social bonds and creates lasting patterns of mutual understanding. His therapeutic work demonstrated the healing effects of social harmony. Patients who participated in harmonious group activities showed improved mental health outcomes. Their brain scans revealed enhanced connectivity between regions associated with empathy and social cognition.

Sacred Spaces in the Brain

Peterson's research identified specific neural patterns associated with experiences of sacred space. His studies showed that when people enter environments they consider sacred, their brains shift into distinctive states characterized by increased alpha waves and reduced stress responses.

These findings helped explain why traditional societies always maintained sacred spaces. His clinical work showed how access to such spaces affects mental health. Patients who regularly spent time in environments they considered sacred showed better psychological outcomes than those who lacked such experiences.

Community Health Markers

At Harvard, Peterson studied the psychological indicators of healthy communities. His research revealed specific patterns that distinguish thriving social groups from struggling ones. These patterns included clear communication channels, fair distribution of responsibilities, and shared commitment to group values.

His clinical observations showed how these elements affect individual mental health. People in well-functioning communities displayed better stress management abilities and stronger psychological resilience. Their neural patterns showed improved integration between emotional and rational brain centers.

Social Learning Networks

Peterson's research demonstrated how communities facilitate learning and development. His studies showed that social groups create networks of shared knowledge that help members acquire new skills and understanding more effectively than they could alone. Through his clinical practice, he observed how these learning networks affect psychological growth. Patients who participated in supportive learning communities showed faster improvement rates and better retention of therapeutic gains than those who worked in isolation.

The Psychology of Group Boundaries

Peterson's work revealed how psychological boundaries function in healthy communities. His research showed that clear, well-maintained boundaries create a sense of safety that allows for optimal brain function and social development.

His clinical observations demonstrated how boundary maintenance affects mental health. Communities with clear, consistent boundaries showed lower rates of interpersonal conflict and higher levels of member satisfaction. Their members displayed better emotional regulation and stronger social skills.

Chapter 9: Navigating Modern Challenges

The Digital Mind

Peterson studied how digital technology affects brain function and psychological development. His research revealed specific patterns in how constant connectivity alters neural pathways. Brain scans showed increased activity in attention-switching areas but decreased activity in regions associated with sustained focus and deep thinking.

His observations of patients demonstrated how technology use affects mental health. Those who maintained healthy boundaries with digital devices showed better psychological outcomes than those who remained constantly connected.

Their brains displayed stronger activation in areas associated with emotional regulation and self-reflection.

Sacred Space in a Digital Age

Peterson's research at Harvard examined how people create and maintain psychological sacred spaces in technological environments. His studies showed that the human brain still requires periods of genuine contemplation and meaningful engagement, despite the constant pull of digital distraction.

His clinical work revealed how different forms of technology use affect psychological well-being. Patients who carved out specific times and spaces for contemplation, free from digital interference, showed improved mental health outcomes. Their brain scans indicated better integration between emotional and cognitive centers.

The Neuroscience of Belief

At McGill University, Peterson studied how religious and secular belief systems affect brain function. His research demonstrated that strong belief systems - whether religious or secular - create similar patterns of neural activation associated with reduced anxiety and increased sense of purpose.

Through his psychological practice, Peterson documented how belief affects mental health in modern contexts. Patients who maintained coherent belief systems showed greater resilience when facing challenges. Their psychological profiles indicated better stress management abilities and stronger social connections.

Adaptation and Mental Health

Peterson's research examined how humans adapt psychologically to rapid social change. His studies showed that successful adaptation requires maintaining certain psychological constants - such as meaningful relationships and purposeful work - while adjusting to new circumstances.

His clinical observations revealed specific patterns in successful adaptation. Patients who balanced technological engagement with traditional forms of meaning-making showed better psychological outcomes. Their neural patterns indicated healthy integration of new experiences with established values.

The Psychology of Modern Meaning

Through his work at the University of Toronto, Peterson studied how people construct meaning in contemporary settings. His research showed that despite technological changes, the basic psychological needs for purpose, connection, and growth remain constant.

His clinical practice demonstrated how these needs manifest in modern life. Patients who found ways to fulfill these fundamental requirements, even in changed circumstances, showed better mental health outcomes. Their brain scans revealed stronger connectivity in regions associated with well-being and purpose.

PART IV: THE PATH FORWARD

Chapter 10: The Integration of Wisdom

The Psychology of Ancient Knowledge

Peterson's research examined how ancient wisdom traditions align with modern psychological findings. His studies showed that traditional practices - from meditation to storytelling - create measurable changes in brain function that support psychological health. These changes include enhanced connectivity between emotional and rational brain centers, improved stress response regulation, and increased activation in areas associated with self-awareness. Through his clinical practice, Peterson documented how ancient wisdom practices affect modern mental health. His patients who incorporated traditional contemplative practices alongside conventional therapy showed faster improvement rates. Their brain scans revealed enhanced integration between different neural networks, suggesting that ancient practices facilitate psychological wholeness in scientifically verifiable ways.

Neural Networks of Understanding

Peterson's research at McGill University focused on how the brain integrates different types of knowledge. His studies revealed that meaningful learning involves multiple brain regions working in concert - emotional centers, memory systems, and rational processing areas all contribute to deep understanding. This finding explained why traditional teaching methods, which engage multiple mental faculties, often prove more effective than purely intellectual approaches. His clinical observations showed how this integration occurs in therapeutic settings. Patients who combined emotional insight with rational understanding demonstrated better outcomes than those who emphasized one approach over the other. Their psychological profiles indicated improved ability to handle life's challenges and maintain stable mental health.

The Science of Meaning Creation

At Harvard, Peterson studied the neurological basis of meaning-making. His research showed that personal meaning emerges from the integration of multiple brain systems - memory, emotion, abstract reasoning, and social understanding all contribute to the experience of meaningfulness. This finding helped explain why isolated intellectual knowledge often fails to create lasting change. Through his therapeutic work, Peterson observed how meaning formation affects mental health. His patients who developed coherent systems of personal meaning showed greater resilience in facing difficulties. Their brain scans revealed increased connectivity between regions associated with purpose and emotional regulation.

Psychological Integration in Practice

Peterson's clinical research demonstrated specific patterns in successful psychological integration. His studies showed that mental health requires balanced development of multiple capacities: emotional awareness, rational thinking, social connection, and moral reasoning. This balance creates measurable changes in brain organization and function.

His observations revealed how integration manifests in daily life. Patients who achieved better psychological integration showed improved relationships, more stable emotional states, and greater life satisfaction. Their neural patterns indicated enhanced communication between different brain regions, suggesting actual physical changes resulting from psychological wholeness.

The Biology of Understanding

Through his research, Peterson identified specific biological markers of integrated understanding. His studies showed that when people genuinely grasp something at multiple levels - intellectual, emotional, and practical - their brains display distinctive patterns of activation. These patterns differ significantly from those seen during mere intellectual comprehension.

His clinical practice provided numerous examples of this process. Patients who developed integrated understanding showed improved ability to handle life challenges. Their brain scans revealed enhanced connectivity between cognitive and emotional centers, indicating true psychological growth.

Sacred Knowledge and Neural Networks

Peterson's research examined how religious and spiritual practices affect brain function. His studies demonstrated that sacred practices create specific patterns of neural activation associated with improved psychological health. These patterns include enhanced connectivity between brain regions associated with meaning, emotion, and self-regulation.

His therapeutic work showed how sacred knowledge integration affects mental health. Patients who incorporated spiritual practices into their lives displayed improved psychological outcomes. Their brain scans showed increased activity in regions associated with well-being and reduced activity in areas linked to anxiety and depression.

The Architecture of Integration

At the University of Toronto, Peterson studied how people build integrated psychological structures. His research revealed that successful integration follows specific patterns: recognition of different types of knowledge, conscious effort to combine them, and practical application in daily life. This process creates measurable changes in brain organization and function. His clinical observations demonstrated the importance of proper sequence in integration. Patients who attempted to skip developmental stages or rush the integration process showed poorer outcomes than those who followed natural developmental sequences. Their psychological profiles indicated the necessity of careful, systematic integration for lasting mental health.

Maintaining Psychological Balance

Peterson's research identified specific factors that support ongoing psychological integration. His studies showed that mental health requires regular attention to multiple aspects of experience: physical health, emotional well-being, social connection, and spiritual or philosophical reflection. This balanced attention creates stable patterns of brain activation associated with psychological health.

Through his clinical practice, Peterson documented how this balance affects daily life. Patients who maintained attention to multiple aspects of experience showed better resilience and life satisfaction. Their neural patterns indicated improved integration between different brain systems, suggesting that balanced attention supports overall psychological health.

Chapter 11: Beyond Wrestling

The Neuroscience of Resolution

At the University of Toronto, Peterson's research examined the brain states associated with psychological resolution. His studies showed how the nervous system shifts after periods of intense struggle, revealing measurable changes in brain chemistry and neural activation patterns. These changes include reduced activity in the amygdala, the brain's fear center, and increased activation in areas associated with calm and clarity.

Through his clinical practice, Peterson documented the physiological markers of genuine peace. His patients who successfully worked through psychological challenges showed distinct changes in their stress response systems. Their cortisol levels decreased, heart rate variability improved, and brain scans revealed enhanced connectivity between emotional regulation centers and higher cognitive areas.

Psychological Equilibrium

Peterson's research at McGill University focused on how people maintain psychological balance after periods of transformation. His studies revealed specific patterns in successful stabilization, showing how the brain reorganizes itself to incorporate new understanding while maintaining functional stability.

His clinical observations demonstrated clear differences between temporary relief and lasting peace. Patients who achieved genuine resolution showed sustained improvements in their psychological measures, while those who found only temporary escape often relapsed into old patterns. The brain scans of those who found lasting peace showed permanent changes in neural organization.

The Biology of Teaching

At Harvard, Peterson studied the neurological basis of effective teaching and mentoring. His research revealed how the brain responds differently when receiving information from a trusted guide versus learning in isolation. This finding helped explain why traditional mentor-student relationships prove so effective in transmitting both knowledge and wisdom. Through his therapeutic practice, Peterson observed how teaching affects both teacher and student. His studies showed increased neural synchronization between individuals during effective teaching interactions, suggesting that meaningful instruction creates actual brain-to-brain coupling between teacher and learner.

Patterns of Growth

Peterson's clinical research identified specific stages in psychological development beyond initial breakthroughs. His studies showed how the brain continues to reorganize itself long after apparent resolution, creating increasingly stable patterns of function and more efficient neural networks.

His observations revealed how this continued growth manifests in daily life. Patients who maintained attention to their psychological development showed ongoing improvements in their mental health measures. Their brain scans indicated increasing integration between different neural systems over time.

The Architecture of Peace

Through his research at the University of Toronto, Peterson examined how lasting peace establishes itself in the brain. His studies showed that genuine psychological peace isn't merely the absence of conflict but rather the presence of well-organized neural systems working in harmony.

His clinical work demonstrated how this peace affects behavior. Patients who achieved true psychological resolution showed improved ability to handle new challenges without falling back into old patterns. Their neural activity indicated better integration between emotional and rational brain centers.

Teaching and Neural Networks

Peterson's research revealed how teaching others strengthens one's own psychological gains. His studies showed that explaining concepts to others creates stronger neural pathways than merely understanding them personally. This finding supported the ancient wisdom that teaching solidifies learning.

Through his clinical practice, Peterson observed how becoming a mentor affects psychological health. Patients who took on teaching roles showed enhanced stability in their own mental health measures. Their brain scans revealed strengthened neural patterns associated with their areas of instruction.

Ongoing Integration

At McGill University, Peterson studied how psychological integration continues after initial breakthroughs. His research showed that the brain continues to optimize its function long after apparent resolution, creating increasingly efficient neural networks and more stable patterns of operation. His clinical observations revealed how this ongoing integration affects daily life. Patients who maintained awareness of their psychological processes showed continuing improvements in their mental health outcomes. Their neural patterns indicated increasing sophistication in handling life's challenges.

The Science of Stability

Peterson's research examined how psychological stability establishes itself over time. His studies showed that true stability isn't rigid but rather represents a flexible, resilient state characterized by efficient neural responses to changing conditions.

Through his therapeutic work, Peterson documented how this stability manifests in behavior. Patients who achieved genuine psychological stability showed improved ability to handle unexpected challenges. Their brain scans revealed enhanced connectivity between different neural networks, indicating better overall system integration.

Chapter 12: The New Dawn

The Science of Personal Change

Through his research at the University of Toronto, Peterson studied the neurological basis of personal transformation. His studies revealed specific patterns in how the brain reorganizes itself during periods of significant change. These patterns include increased neural plasticity, enhanced connectivity between different brain regions, and measurable changes in neurotransmitter production.

His clinical practice provided extensive documentation of how transformation occurs in real situations. Patients who achieved lasting personal change showed consistent alterations in their brain function. Their neural scans revealed new patterns of activation, suggesting that genuine transformation creates actual physical changes in brain structure.

Social Networks and Change

At McGill University, Peterson's research examined how individual changes affect social groups. His studies showed that when one person undergoes significant psychological development, their transformation creates measurable effects in their social network. These effects include altered patterns of group interaction and changes in collective behavior.

Through his therapeutic work, Peterson observed how personal growth influences others. His patients who achieved substantial psychological development often reported similar changes beginning to occur in their families and close associates. Brain scans of social groups showed synchronized patterns of neural activation among members.

The Biology of Social Impact

Peterson's research at Harvard focused on how individual transformation affects group dynamics at a biological level. His studies revealed that when people change in meaningful ways, they create new patterns of social interaction that affect the nervous systems of those around them. This finding helped explain how personal growth can catalyze broader social change.

His clinical observations demonstrated these effects in action. Patients who maintained their psychological gains showed an increased ability to influence positive changes in their social circles. Their presence created measurable changes in the stress responses and emotional states of others.

Psychological Stability and Growth

Through his work at the University of Toronto, Peterson studied how people maintain psychological gains while continuing to develop. His research showed that successful growth requires a balance between stability and flexibility - too much rigidity prevents development, while too much change creates instability.

His clinical practice revealed how this balance manifests in behavior. Patients who found the right mix of stability and growth showed better long-term outcomes. Their brain scans indicated optimal integration between conservation and adaptation networks in the brain.

The Architecture of Change

Peterson's research identified specific patterns in successful psychological transformation. His studies showed that lasting change follows predictable neurological sequences, creating increasingly stable patterns of brain function while maintaining adaptability.

Through his clinical work, Peterson documented how these patterns affect behavior. Patients who followed natural developmental sequences showed better outcomes than those who attempted to force change. Their psychological profiles indicated more stable and lasting improvements.

Teaching and Transformation

At Harvard, Peterson studied how teaching affects psychological development. His research showed that helping others understand and grow creates reciprocal benefits, strengthening neural patterns associated with personal development in both teacher and student.

His clinical observations revealed how teaching accelerates personal growth. Patients who took on mentoring roles showed enhanced stability in their own psychological gains. Their brain scans indicated strengthened neural patterns associated with their areas of instruction.

The Future of Development

Peterson's research revealed specific factors that support ongoing psychological growth. His studies showed that continued development requires regular engagement with meaningful challenges, strong social connections, and consistent attention to personal values.

Through his clinical practice, Peterson observed how these factors affect long-term outcomes. Patients who maintained attention to their development showed sustained improvement in their mental health measures. Their neural patterns indicated increasing sophistication in handling life's challenges.

Social Evolution and Growth

At McGill University, Peterson studied how psychological development affects social evolution. His research showed that when individuals grow in healthy ways, they create new patterns of social interaction that support collective development.

His clinical work demonstrated these effects in action. Patients who achieved significant personal growth often became catalysts for positive change in their communities. Their presence created measurable improvements in group functioning and social cohesion.

Epilogue: The Eternal Dance

The Psychology of Growth

Through twenty years of clinical practice at the University of Toronto, Peterson observed consistent patterns in psychological development. His research revealed how the human brain continues to change and adapt throughout life, creating new neural pathways and strengthening existing ones. These changes occur most dramatically during periods of conscious psychological work, but they continue subtly even during times of apparent stability.

His studies showed that mental growth follows natural rhythms - periods of intense change followed by periods of integration. Brain scans of patients in different stages of development revealed how these rhythms manifest in neural activity. During change phases, the brain shows increased plasticity and new pattern formation. During integration phases, these patterns stabilize and strengthen.

The Dance of Development

At McGill University, Peterson's research examined the interplay between stability and change in psychological growth. His studies demonstrated how successful development requires both movement and rest, much like a dance. The brain needs periods of active reorganization followed by periods of consolidation.

Through his clinical observations, Peterson documented how this dance affects mental health. Patients who worked with these natural rhythms showed better outcomes than those who attempted to force constant change. Their psychological profiles indicated improved stability and enhanced ability to handle life's challenges.

Seeds of Tomorrow

Peterson's research at Harvard focused on how current changes affect future development. His studies showed that each step in psychological growth creates new possibilities for further development. This finding helped explain why personal transformation often accelerates over time.

His clinical practice provided numerous examples of this acceleration. Patients who achieved initial breakthroughs often found subsequent changes easier to accomplish. Their brain scans revealed increasingly efficient patterns of adaptation and integration.

The Call Forward

At the University of Toronto, Peterson studied how people respond to opportunities for growth. His research revealed specific patterns in successful responses to life's calls for development. These patterns include increased neural activation in areas associated with courage and decision-making.

Through his therapeutic work, Peterson observed how different people handle these calls. Those who responded positively showed enhanced psychological outcomes and improved life satisfaction. Their neural patterns indicated better integration between emotional and rational brain centers.

Cycles of Change

Peterson's research identified recurring patterns in psychological development. His studies showed how growth moves through predictable phases, each building upon previous achievements while opening new possibilities. This understanding helped explain both individual and social transformation.

His clinical observations revealed how these cycles manifest in real life. Patients who understood and worked with these natural patterns showed better outcomes in their psychological development. Their brain scans indicated improved neural organization and enhanced adaptive capabilities.

The Future Beckons

Through his research at McGill University, Peterson examined how current psychological understanding creates new possibilities for human development. His studies showed that as people gain better understanding of mental processes, they become more capable of directed psychological growth.

His clinical practice demonstrated these possibilities in action. Patients who combined scientific understanding with personal insight showed enhanced rates of psychological development. Their neural patterns revealed increasingly sophisticated responses to life's challenges. The scientific evidence gathered through Peterson's decades of research and clinical practice points toward expanding possibilities for human psychological development. As our understanding of mental processes grows, so too does our ability to work effectively with them. This knowledge, combined with the wisdom of traditional practices, opens new frontiers in human potential.

These findings suggest that the eternal dance between struggle and growth, between movement and rest, continues to shape human development. The patterns observed in Peterson's research and clinical practice indicate that this dance remains as relevant today as it was in ancient times, though our understanding of its mechanisms has grown more sophisticated.

The evidence shows that each person who engages seriously in this process of growth adds to our collective understanding. Each breakthrough, each insight, each step forward contributes to the growing body of knowledge about human psychological development. This accumulation of understanding creates new possibilities for those who follow.

The End.